2011

Enjoy This Book!

Manage your library account and
discover all we offer by visiting us
online at www.nashualibrary.org.

Please return this book on time
so others can enjoy it, too.

If you love what your
library offers, tell a friend!

@ **Nashua Public Library**
2 Court Street, Nashua, NH 03060
603-589-4600, www.nashualibrary.org

J

Taylor Swift

By Lynn Peppas

Crabtree Publishing Company

www.crabtreebooks.com

Crabtree Publishing Company
www.crabtreebooks.com

Author: Lynn Peppas
Publishing plan research and development:
  Sean Charlebois, Reagan Miller
  Crabtree Publishing Company
Project coordinator: Kathy Middleton
Photo research: Crystal Sikkens
Editor: Molly Aloian
Proofreader and Indexer: Wendy Scavuzzo
Designer: Ken Wright
Production coordinator and Prepress technician: Ken Wright

Photographs:
Associated Press: page 25
Corbis: © Andrew Orth/Retna Ltd.: pages 9,
  10, 13, 14, 16, 17; © John G. Mabanglo/epa:
  page 12; Danny Moloshok/Reuters: page 21
Dreamstime: page 4
Keystone Press: © Mark Chilton-Richfoto/
  zumapress: page 5; © Jason Moore/zumapress:
  pages 6, 18, 19; © Randi Radcliff/AdMedia:
  page 11; © Santana, Luis/zumapress: page 22;
  © FOTOS International: page 23; © JMS/
  wenn.com: page 24; © FAME pictures: page 26;
  © New Line Cinema/zumapress: page 27;
  © EMPICS Entertainment: page 28
Retna Pictures: page 1; George Chin: cover
Shutterstock: page 7
Wikipedia: Ed!: page 15; David Shankbone:
  page 20

Library and Archives Canada Cataloguing in Publication

Peppas, Lynn
   Taylor Swift / by Lynn Peppas.

(Superstars!)
Includes index.
Also available in an electronic format.
ISBN 978-0-7787-7252-1 (bound).--ISBN 978-0-7787-7261-3 (pbk.)

   1. Swift, Taylor, 1989- --Juvenile literature. 2. Country musicians--United States--Biography--Juvenile literature.
I. Title. II. Series: Superstars! (St. Catharines, Ont.)

ML3930.S989P42 2011   j782.421642092   C2010-905305-2

Library of Congress Cataloging-in-Publication Data

Peppas, Lynn.
Taylor Swift / by Lynn Peppas.
   p. cm. -- (Superstars!)
Includes index.
ISBN 978-0-7787-7261-3 (pbk. : alk. paper) --
ISBN 978-0-7787-7252-1 (reinforced library binding : alk. paper) --
ISBN 978-1-4271-9557-9 (electronic pdf : alk. paper)
1. Swift, Taylor, 1989---Juvenile literature. 2. Women country musicians--United States--Biography--Juvenile literature. I. Title.
ML3930.S989P46 2011
782.421642092--dc22
[B]
                                    2010032492

Crabtree Publishing Company
www.crabtreebooks.com   1-800-387-7650

Printed in the USA/102010/SP20100915

Published in Canada
Crabtree Publishing
616 Welland Ave.
St. Catharines, ON
L2M 5V6

Published in the United States
Crabtree Publishing
PMB 59051
350 Fifth Avenue, 59th Floor
New York, New York 10118

Published in the United Kingdom
Crabtree Publishing
Maritime House
Basin Road North, Hove
BN41 1WR

Published in Australia
Crabtree Publishing
386 Mt. Alexander Rd.
Ascot Vale (Melbourne)
VIC 3032

CONTENTS

Words that are defined in the glossary are in
bold type the first time they appear in the text.

Who Is Taylor Swift?

American singer and songwriter Taylor Swift started her career in music at the young age of ten. A strong-minded young woman who knew what she wanted, she worked hard and never gave up. It took her less than six years to make her dream come true. Today, she is the first country music artist to win an MTV Video Music award, and have a country pop song hit number one on Top 40 Radio list.

She Said It

When I get news [that I'm the top-selling artist of 2008], it just blows my mind, because I've been trying to do this all my life. I remember the girls who would come to talent shows and say to anyone they met, 'I'm so-and-so. I'm going to be famous someday.' I was never that girl. I would show up with my guitar and say, 'This is a song I wrote about a boy in my class.' And that's what I still do today."
—Interview in *Glamour* magazine, August 2009

Humble Beginnings

Taylor began at the bottom of the ladder of success. She sang at local sports events and **karaoke** bars in Pennsylvania while growing up. By the age of 12, she began writing her own songs. Jump ahead just a few years and, by 2008, more people were buying her albums than any other recording artist in the world!

Taylor Swift poses with her MTV Best Female Video award in 2009.

Model and Designer

Taylor's talents as a singer and songwriter prove that she is certainly not just another pretty face. But, let's face it, the 5'11" (180 cm) tall, blonde-haired beauty has the look for fashion **runways** and magazines. In fact, she's a familiar face on the cover of American music and fashion magazines. She graduated from working as a model for L.e.i. to designing her own sundresses with L.e.i. for Walmart in 2009.

From the Heart

Taylor is known for writing songs straight from the heart. Many of her **lyrics** are about personal experiences and events. Her songs explore emotions such as love, anger, and uncertainty, and difficult experiences such as betrayal. She writes about real-life situations, such as having secret crushes and meeting a new guy or breaking-up with a boyfriend. Her first hit song "Tim McGraw" was about hoping an ex-boyfriend would think of her when their special song by the country singer Tim McGraw was played.

She Said It

"People who have no idea that I have a crush on them won't find out through me telling them, but they will find out when they hear their name in a song. There was this guy who opened a couple of shows for me on tour and I talked to him a couple of times, but he never knew that I liked him. So I wrote this song called "Hey Stephen," and when my album came out, I sent him a text message: 'Hey, Track 5'"
—Interview in The New York Times article *"Little Miss Sunshine,"* December 2009

She Said It

*"For me, those are the people that I looked to, and those are the reasons why I fell in love with country music...The fans are a huge reason, but also going back to my **inspiration** and the reason why I wanted to do this—Shania and Garth. They're just unbelievable artists..."*
—Interview on CMT.com, June 2009

Country singer LeAnn Rimes was one of Taylor Swift's big inspirations.

Inspirations

Taylor Swift first fell in love with country music when she heard LeAnn Rimes singing "Blue" on TV. Taylor was ten years old at the time. While accepting her CMT (Country Music Television) award for video of the year in 2009, Taylor said she was also inspired by other country-singing superstars such as Garth Brooks and Shania Twain.

Growing Up Taylor Swift

Taylor Alison Swift was born on December 13, 1989, in Wyomissing—a **suburb** of Reading, Pennsylvania. Taylor's parents Scott and Andrea Swift decided to name her "Taylor" so people wouldn't judge her by her **gender**. Today, most people know Taylor Swift is a young woman because of her fame as a recording artist.

OPERA GRANNY!

Taylor's parents are both talented businesspeople. So where did her singing talent come from? Taylor's grandmother, on her mother's side, was an **opera** singer and recording artist in Puerto Rico.

Down on the Farm

Taylor grew up on her parents' farm in Wyomissing. When she was two years old, her parents had another child, Taylor's younger brother Austin. Scott Swift worked as a financial adviser for Merrill Lynch while Taylor was growing up. A financial adviser is someone who gives people advice on how to use their money to make, or save, even more money. Andrea Swift worked at an advertising agency before she had Taylor. She quit her job so she could stay at home to raise her children. Andrea worked on the farm and grew Christmas trees to sell during the holiday season. Taylor's song "The Best Day" is about her close relationship with her mom and dad and how they've always turned her worst days into her best days.

She Said It

"I know that a Christmas tree farm in Pennsylvania is about the most random place for a country singer to come from but I had an awesome childhood. We had horses and cats, and my mom stayed home with me. Our dad would come home from work and then go outside to make a split-rail fence."
—Interview in *Women's Health* magazine, August 2009

Four-year-old Taylor riding fences in Pennsylvania

Talented Three-Year-Old

Taylor's parents recognized their little girl's talents for memorizing lyrics at a very early age. Taylor recalled the story her parents told her about the three of them driving home after seeing the Disney movie *The Little Mermaid*. Taylor was sitting in the backseat of the car singing the words to the songs she had just heard. Her parents were amazed that Taylor could remember all the words!

She Said It

"My grandmother was an opera singer, and so she was always singing, either around the house, or every single Sunday she'd get up and sing in front of the entire congregation at church."
—Interview on CMT.com, November 26, 2008

Starting School

Taylor and her brother went to Wyndcroft School in Pottstown, Pennsylvania. Taylor's favorite subjects were English and creative writing. Her favorite children's authors when she was a child were Shel Silverstein and Dr. Seuss. Both of these authors are known for using rhymes in their books and poems. Today, Taylor uses rhyme in her own songwriting.

A Move to Musicals

Taylor's mom got her involved in a local children's community theater group in Wyomissing, Pennsylvania, when she was nine years old. Taylor loved acting, especially in musicals. She played the lead role of Sandy in the stage musical *Grease*. It was during her performance in this musical that she decided to pursue a career in country music.

Taylor Swift with mom and brother

She Said It

*"I would read the Shel Silverstein poems, Dr. Seuss, and I noticed early on that poetry was something that just stuck in my head, and I was replaying those rhymes and [trying] to think of my own. In English, the only thing I wanted to do was poetry and all the other kids were like, 'Oh man. We have to write poems again?' and I would have a three-page-long poem. I won a **national** poetry contest when I was in fourth grade for a poem called 'Monster in My Closet.'"*
—Interview on RollingStone.com, December 2008

Getting Heard

At ten years old, Taylor was willing to go almost anywhere to be heard onstage. She began doing karaoke and won a karaoke competition at the Pat Garrett Roadhouse in Strausstown, Pennsylvania. She won the chance to be the opening act for a Charlie Daniels concert.

Taylor realized that performing the national anthem for sports games was another good way to be heard. When she was 11 years old, she sang the anthem at a Philadelphia 76ers basketball game. The famous American hip hop musician Jay-Z was in the audience. He was so impressed by her performance that he high-fived Taylor as she made her way back to her seat.

Taylor still enjoys singing the national anthem at sports games.

Taylor's First Demo CD

Taylor knew she wanted to be a country singing star. She also knew that people in the music business would have to hear her to believe in her talent. At the age of 11, she and her mother recorded a **demo** CD of Taylor singing karaoke country songs. They took the CD to Nashville, Tennessee. Taylor passed out copies of her demo to different record labels on Music Row, a famous street in Nashville where many record labels are. But nobody called her back. It was back to singing the national anthem for Taylor.

One, Two, Three

At 12 years old, Taylor learned to play her first three chords on guitar from a computer technician who was fixing Taylor's computer. On that very same day she wrote her first song called "Lucky You."

Taylor knew at a very young age that she wanted to be a country music performer.

She Said It

"I would literally play [guitar] until my fingers bled, my mom had to tape them up, and you can imagine how popular that made me: 'Look at her fingers, so weird.' ...But for the first time, I could sit in class and those girls could say anything they wanted about me, because after school I was going to go home and write a song about it."
—Interview on RollingStone.com, February 2009

High School

Taylor started writing songs soon after starting Wyomissing Area Junior/Senior High School. She didn't have many friends at the school and felt like an "outsider" partly because she spent a lot of her time performing in karaoke bars. She called it a "very lonely time in my life." She used the emotions she felt to write the song "Lucky You," about a girl who is different and doesn't fit in.

13

Swift Rise to Fame

When Taylor was 13 years old, she sang the national anthem at the U.S. Open, the biggest tennis championship in the United States. A person in the entertainment business was impressed by her performance. They set her up to meet music manager Dan Dymtrow. Dan was a successful manager for Britney Spears at the time. He became Taylor's manager, too. It was the first big step in Taylor's career!

RCA Takes Notice

One of the first official jobs Dan got Taylor was not as a singer but as a model. Taylor modeled for Abercrombie & Fitch's Rising Stars **advertising campaign** at 13 years old.

Taylor Swift at age 14

Dan also had Taylor record a demo CD of her best original songs. RCA heard it and offered her a development deal. This meant they would pay Taylor to record some of her music but they did not promise to release her album(s). Taylor and her family knew this could be the big break she was looking for. The family moved closer to Nashville, so their daughter could make her country music dream come true. They moved to Hendersonville, a suburb of Nashville, Tennessee, on Old Hickory Lake.

Taylor's BFF

Taylor started attending Hendersonville High School. It was here that she met her best friend Abigail Lauren Anderson. One thing the two friends had in common was their love for the movie *Napoleon Dynamite*.

Hendersonville High School

She Said It

"I didn't want to be just another girl singer. I wanted there to be something that set me apart. And I knew that had to be my [song] writing."
—Interview in *Entertainment Weekly*, July 2007

Moving On to Sony

After one year at RCA, Taylor felt her music career wasn't moving as quickly as she wanted. RCA wanted Taylor to start recording other people's songs. Taylor wanted to write and sing her own songs. She decided to leave RCA.

Taylor took an offer from Sony/ATV Music Publishing. She didn't get a recording deal but got a job writing music for the company instead. That was okay by Taylor. At 14 years old, she became the youngest house writer in Sony/ATV history.

She Said It

"I absolutely can't stop writing songs. It's funny because sometimes you'll hear artists talking about how they have to hurry up and write this next record, and it's like, I can't stop writing. I can't turn it off. I go through situations and I go through experiences and I go through life and I need to write it. I need to write it down."
—Interview on RollingStone.com, December 2008

Big Machine Records

Taylor was writing music after school at Sony/ATV and performing her songs wherever she could. One of her performances was at the Bluebird Café in Nashville. Scott Borchetta went to see Taylor perform. He was planning to launch his own record label Big Machine Records and wanted Taylor to record an album. She signed a record deal with Scott in the fall of 2005. They began working on her **debut** record right away.

Taylor Swift performing in January 2004

16

A Hit on MySpace

Taylor couldn't wait for her debut album to come out. In December 2005, she decided to make her own MySpace account so her friends and fans could hear her songs. She uploaded tracks from her soon-to-be released debut album. She had over 2 million hits on her account before her album was released. Since its release, Taylor has had more MySpace visits than any other country artist on MySpace, and made the top 15 most-visited artists in any music **genre**.

FIRST HIT SINGLE

Taylor wrote "Tim McGraw" with Liz Rose while at Sony/ATV. It became Taylor's first single and was released on June 19, 2006. It made the number 6 spot on the U.S. Billboard Hot Country Songs chart. Since its release, it has sold over 3 million copies.

Taylor Swift

Taylor's debut album *Taylor Swift* was released in October 2006. All the songs on the album were written, or co-written, by Taylor. The album was almost entirely produced by Nathan Chapman, someone she'd worked with at Sony. The album has two number one hits, "Our Song" and "Should've Said No." Other hit songs from the album include "Tim McGraw," "Teardrops on My Guitar," and "Picture to Burn." The album holds the record for being the longest charting album by a female country artist on the U.S. Billboard 200. By January 2010, the album had sold over 4 million copies.

First Tour for Taylor

Taylor did not return to high school in September 2006. Instead, she chose to be homeschooled so she could focus on her music career. After the release of *Taylor Swift*, she went on tour opening for the Rascal Flatts' Me and My Gang tour. In 2007, she toured with other country music stars including George Strait, Brad Paisley, and Kenny Chesney. She even went on tour with her first hit single's namesake Tim McGraw and his country superstar wife Faith Hill. Her first tour lasted for more than one year!

Taylor lives her dream and goes on her first tour. She opened for a number of country music stars in 2007.

Sweet 16

Taylor Swift was making her dreams come true. At 16 years old, she had just released her debut album. It reached platinum in less than one year. Her music was topping the charts. In 2007 alone, she was nominated for many awards. She won a BMI (Broadcast Music, Inc.) award for Winning Song for "Tim McGraw," the Horizon award from the Country Music Association, and Breakthrough Video of the Year at the CMT Music awards. The Nashville Songwriters Association also awarded her Songwriter/Artist of the Year. Taylor was swiftly moving toward superstardom!

Taylor won the 2007 CMT Music Award for Breakthrough Video of the Year for the video "Tim McGraw."

He Said It

"For [Taylor] to have written that record at 16, it's crazy how good it is. I figured I'd hear it and think, 'Well, it's good for 16'—but it's just flat-out good for any age."
—Brad Paisley, on EW.com, July 2007

19

Taylor-Made Success

Taylor has grown up from a teenager to a young woman during her music career. Today, she writes the songs that top music charts, sells

more records than any other artist, and she's won over 50 awards for her efforts (and she's only just started her career)! She's the perfect cover girl for fashion and music magazines and is making her way into acting. In 2009, *Forbes* business magazine reported that she'd earned 18 million dollars and listed her as one of the top 100 celebrities of the year. Taylor Swift has made it to superstardom.

Time magazine listed Taylor as one of the 100 most influential people in the world.

More Taylor Swift Records

Taylor's Christmas album, *Sounds of the Season*, was released in October 2007. A few weeks later, she released a CD/DVD called *Taylor Swift: Deluxe Limited Edition*. The new release had a few new songs, such as "I'm Only Me When I'm With You," and Taylor's first phone conversation with Tim McGraw. The DVD also features videos, live performances, and even Taylor's home movie. In July 2008, she released an exclusive **EP** at Walmart stores called *Beautiful Eyes* with two new songs. The EP reached the number one spot on the U.S. Billboard Top Country Album chart.

"This is my life's goal…To have a song on Grey's Anatomy. *My love of* Grey's Anatomy *has never wavered. It's my longest relationship to date."*
—Interview on ETonline.com, September 2008

Fearless

Taylor released her second full-length album *Fearless* on November 11, 2008. It debuted at number one on the Billboard 200 chart, and sold over half a million copies in its first week of sales. It became the best-selling country album in digital history. Before *Fearless*, Taylor's debut album *Taylor Swift* held the number one spot!

In 2008, when *Fearless* became the number one country record, Taylor's first album was still on the chart in the number 6 position. That meant she had not one, but two albums on the Billboard 200 Album chart. It also meant that Taylor sold more albums than any other artist in the United States!

TAYLOR TV

One of Taylor's favorite TV shows is *Grey's Anatomy* on ABC. She admitted that she began crying when she got the phone call saying they were going to use her song "White Horse" (from her *Fearless* album) on the 2008 premiere for the show.

Fearless won Album of the Year at the 52nd Grammy Awards in January 2010.

She Said It

"So many girls come up and say to me, 'I have never listened to country music in my life. I didn't even know my town had a country-music station. Then I got your record, and now I'm obsessed.' That's the coolest compliment to me."
—Interview on Time.com, April 2009

CROSSOVER

Taylor's music has introduced a new generation of young listeners to country music. It has also made the crossover to pop rock. Taylor's song "Love Song" was the first country song to make Nielsen's BDS Top 40 chart.

He Said It

"If I haven't said it yet today, thank God for Taylor Swift...By the end of the year, or at some point within the next 12 months, we're going to be looking at 10 million albums sold before we get to album three."
—Scott Borchetta, Big Machine Records executive producer, in *Billboard* magazine, July 2009

Dating Joe Jonas

In the summer of 2008, when Taylor was 18 years old, she dated Joe Jonas of the Jonas Brothers. In November 2008, on *Ellen* she explained to Ellen DeGeneres that they had recently broken up. Taylor wrote about her and Joe's break-up in the song "Forever & Always." Big Machine Records allowed Taylor a "last minute" recording session so she could get her latest song on the album.

Taylor performs with the Jonas Brothers (left to right: Nick, Joe, and Kevin) in January 2008.

She Said It

"Someday I'm going to find somebody really, really great who's right for me…And when I look at that person I'm not even going to be able to remember the boy who broke up with me over the phone in 25 seconds when I was 18. It was a record, I think, for how quick—I looked at the call log and it was 27 seconds."
—On *Ellen*, November 2008

Fearless Tour

Taylor headlined her first tour called Taylor Swift Fearless 2009 in April of that year. The tour went worldwide. She performed concerts in the United States, Canada, Australia, and the United Kingdom. The tour continued into 2010 and was one of the hottest-selling tickets on the concert circuit. Her show at Madison Square Garden in New York City sold out in less than one minute—that's over 300 tickets per second!

Winning Moments in 2009

With Taylor's second successful album release, the awards quickly followed. In 2009, she was nominated for many awards, and won quite a few of them. She won two Academy of Country Music Awards, one for best album. She cleaned up at the American Music Awards, taking home Artist of the Year, Favorite Pop/Rock Female Artist, Favorite Country Female Artist, and Favorite Country Album. At the Billboard Music Awards, she won in seven categories including Artist of the Year. She has won five BMI awards, five Country Music Association awards, two CMT Music awards, two Teen Choice awards—the list of awards from around the world is almost endless.

A glamorous Taylor performs on her 2009 tour.

Taylor and Kanye

Taylor's most talked-about award was her 2009 MTV Video Music award for Best Female Video. During her acceptance speech, hip hop artist Kanye West grabbed the microphone from Taylor and told the audience that Beyoncé had one of the best videos of all time. Taylor was too upset to finish her speech. Later, Beyoncé won the Video of the Year award but, instead of making a speech, called Taylor up so she could finish hers. Kanye West apologized publicly on *The Jay Leno Show* and to Taylor on the phone later. The following year at the 2010 MTV VMA's, Taylor performed her new song "Innocent," which many saw as her way of forgiving Kanye.

She Said It

"I remember being 17 years old up for my first MTV award with Destiny's Child and it was one of the most exciting moments in my life. So I'd like for Taylor to come out and have her moment."
—Beyoncé, at the 2009 MTV Video Music Awards

Taylor's Big-Screen Debut

Taylor-mania had officially hit. The new singing star was in demand for appearances. Her first guest appearance on TV was playing "Haley Jones" on the hit show *CSI* in March 2009. She also sang "Crazier" in *Hannah Montana: The Movie*, released in April 2009. Then on November 7, she hosted *Saturday Night Live* as both the actor and musical guest.

Rapping It Up Taylor-Style

During the CMT awards in November 2009, Taylor (also known as T-Swizzle) and rapper T-Pain showed their video clip of the rap song "Thug Story." It is a **spoof** on Taylor's hit song "Love Story." In the song, Taylor raps about baking cookies and not owning a gun. Taylor's mom even made an appearance on the video.

A Tale of Two Taylors

Twilight star Taylor Lautner and Taylor Swift became very close friends during the filming of the movie *Valentine's Day*. When she hosted *SNL*, Taylor hinted that the two were dating and threw out a kiss to Taylor during her musical monologue. However, the romance was short-lived due to their busy schedules. The couple broke up near the end of December 2009. She hinted that she'll write about their romance in songs on her next album.

Taylor and Taylor in the movie *Valentine's Day*

Valentine's Day

Taylor made her move to the big screen in the romantic comedy *Valentine's Day*, which opened in movie theaters on February 11, 2010. The movie includes many well-known actors such as Julia Roberts, Jamie Foxx, and Ashton Kutcher. The movie is about the relationships between a group of people and how they find romance on Valentine's Day.

Of course, Taylor couldn't just act in the movie. She wrote two songs that are included in the movie soundtrack, "Today Was a Fairytale" and "Jump Then Fall."

Taylor shares a scene with actress Jennifer Garner in *Valentine's Day*.

She Said It

"Hopefully when my next record comes out, it will be like my diary…Writing songs about guys is about as bold as it gets for me."
—Interview in *GL (Girl's Life)* magazine, February/March 2010

She Said It

"Now that things are going pretty well, it's looking like [music] is going to be something I'm doing for a while. I'm crossing my fingers for that. If not, I'll go back to school or I'll just be a songwriter."
—Interview on OKmagazine.com, November 2009

The Future's So Bright

Taylor's third album *Speak Now* will be released in October 2010. Fans got a taste of it with the release of the first single "Mine" in August. In a recent interview in *Rolling Stone* magazine, Taylor says, "Each song is a different confession to a person." And now that Taylor is officially entering her 20s, she's also looking forward to moving into her own apartment in Nashville. She's living her dream and is doing what she loves to do best: make music.

Dressed to impress at the Songwriters Hall of Fame, Taylor receives the Hal David Starlight Award. The award is for songwriters who are making an impact on the music industry.

She Said It

"I don't feel as if I need to make some giant statement and start wearing a completely different new wardrobe for the next project or start speaking in a different way or writing songs in a different way. When you start overthinking that stuff with your career, you stop being who you are and start being who you think you should be. And when you get into that space, that's very dangerous territory. So I'm just going to continue to be who I am."
—Interview in *InStyle* magazine, December 2009

Timeline

1989: Taylor Alison Swift is born on December 13 in Wyomissing, Pennsylvania.

2000: Joins a local children's community theater.

2000: Wins a karaoke contest and gets to open for The Charlie Daniels Band.

2001: Records her first demo CD with her mom's help and shops it around in Nashville.

2001: Sings the national anthem at a Philadelphia 76ers game. Jay-Z high-fives her in the stands.

2003: Taylor signs a development deal with RCA Records. The family moves to Hendersonville.

2004: In the fall, Taylor leaves RCA. Takes a songwriting job at Sony/ATV Music Publishing.

2005: Signs record deal with Scott Borchetta of Big Machine Records in the fall.

2005: In December, Taylor makes her own MySpace account that features her songs.

2006: First single "Tim McGraw" is released in June.

2006: Debut album *Taylor Swift* is released in October.

2006–2007: Starts touring in November, opening for Rascal Flatts' Me and My Gang tour. Also tours with George Strait, Brad Paisley, Kenny Chesney, and Tim McGraw and Faith Hill.

2007: Releases Christmas CD *Sounds of the Season: The Taylor Swift Holiday Collection* in October.

2007: Releases CD/DVD *Taylor Swift: Deluxe Limited Edition* in November.

2008: The EP *Beautiful Eyes* is released to be sold exclusively at Walmart stores in July.

2008: Second album *Fearless* released in November.

2009: Taylor Swift Fearless 2009 tour begins in April.

2009: Hosts *Saturday Night Live* in November.

2010: First film *Valentine's Day* is released in February.

2010: Third album *Speak Now* is due for release in October. The single "Mine" is released in August.

Glossary

advertising campaign A series of efforts to market or sell a product

debut The first artistic release of music or a performance

demo Short for demonstration; a brief tape that showcases a performer's abilities

EP Short form for "extended play": a record that has more songs than a single which contains two songs; an EP usually has four to six songs

gender Being categorized as male or female

genre A classification or type of music, art, or writing that shows a particular style

inspiration Something or someone that influences or motivates a person

karaoke Performing music accompanied by an entertainment system that plays the music and displays the lyrics for popular songs

lyrics Words to a song

national Referring to a nation, such as the United States of America

opera A theatrical style of music that features performers with powerful singing voices

runway A pathway; in the modeling industry, a runway is the long path-like stage where models walk to show the latest fashions

spoof A skit that makes fun of something or someone

suburb A residential area just outside of a large town or city

Find Out More

Books

Bloom, Ronny. *Get the Scoop: Taylor Swift.*
   New York: Price Stern Sloan, 2009.
Shea, Mary Molly. *Country Music Stars: Taylor Swift.*
   New York: Gareth Stevens Publishing, 2010.
Hansen, Amy Gail. *Taylor Swift: Love Story.*
   Chicago, IL: Triumph Books, 2010.

Websites

Taylor Swift
   www.taylorswift.com
The official website of country pop singer
Taylor Swift

Taylor Swift on Myspace
   www.myspace.com/taylorswift
The official myspace page of Taylor Swift,
which features samples of her music

Big Machine Records
   http://bigmachinerecords.com/taylorswift/
Find out the latest album and tour information
on Big Machine Records' website.

Index

About the Author

Lynn Peppas is a writer of children's nonfiction books. She has always been a bookworm and grew up reading all the books she could. She feels fortunate to have been able to combine her love of reading and her love of kids into a career. Her work in children's publishing is a dream-job come true.